THE BONDAGE MAKERS

HOW THE UNBIBLICAL
SPIRITUAL WARFARE MOVEMENT
IS
ENSLAVING BELIEVERS

Ignacio Rovirosa

Copyright © 2006 by Ignacio Rovirosa

The Bondage Makers
by Ignacio Rovirosa

Printed in the United States of America

ISBN 1-60034-274-4

All rights reserved solely by the author. The author guarantees all contents are original and do not infringe upon the legal rights of any other person or work. No part of this book may be reproduced in any form without the permission of the author. The views expressed in this book are not necessarily those of the publisher.

www.xulonpress.com

This book is dedicated
to all those who have suffered
due to the unbiblical teaching
of Spiritual Warfare and to
our very special friends
who experienced the pain with us.
You all know who you are.
And to my wife and children
who paid a great price as well
because I chose to take a stand .
The Lord used you all
to give our family strength
during those trying times.
It is for you
and others like you
that this book was written.
May it be used
to deliver others
as well from the
so-called "deliverance" ministries.

CONTENTS

Introduction ix

Chapter 1 - Sharing Personal Experiences of Spiritual Warfare 11

Chapter 2 – A Play on Words
Biblical Spiritual Warfare vs. Modern Day
Spiritual Warfare 17

Chapter 3 – Who Can and Who Cannot be "Demonized" 35

Chapter 4 – The Devil Made Me Do It 51

Chapter 5 - An Epidemic and The Real Enemy 57

Chapter 6 - The Cure and The Consequences....................63

Conclusion 73

Bibliography 75

INTRODUCTION

In November of 2000, an event occurred that would raise serious questions regarding the spiritual and physical security of a believer. In Kansas City, Missouri, a pastor's wife would take the life of her adult daughter and then proceed to take her own life. All this would occur as a result of today's so-called spiritual warfare movement.

This event would forever alter the lives of the hurting relatives and friends of the deceased, but would also begin my personal research into this unbiblical teaching. Due to this event, as a staff member of this church, I was forced to re-evaluate what I was being taught regarding spiritual warfare. I was being taught this by my pastor.

I want to express that the most difficult thing to do was to confront my pastor regarding this teaching as I had the greatest love for him, but I felt (as I still do today) that my first and foremost allegiance is to God's Word. My desire is not to personally attack anyone who believes in and practices what they call spiritual warfare, but to confront and expose an erroneous belief system that is not only detrimental to a believer's spiritual growth, but also to the physical, emotional, and mental well being of that believer. Many times this belief system also erroneously deals with un-believers as though they were believers thus deceiving them in the issue of their salvation.

I wish to believe that those who follow the modern day spiritual warfare movement are well meaning. They are sincere - yet sincerely wrong. I once practiced this teaching while I was being trained in my local church and to my own shame, sought man's wisdom over God's. I believe that this is still where the errors lie in that movement.

I do believe that true spiritual warfare as explained in the Scriptures is valid when viewed Scripturally. But what these people practice is not spiritual warfare but channeling as well as other unbiblical practices. The purpose of this book is to expose and address the erroneous views taught and practiced by many in today's spiritual warfare movement.

A few years ago a book was written by Neil Anderson promoting spiritual warfare titled "The Bondage Breaker". I submit to you that in reality this teaching is quite the opposite. What has been created due to this teaching are Bondage Makers. Over the last 5 years, the Lord has brought many across my path who have experienced heartaches due to this teaching. Churches have been split, relationships damaged, faiths doubted, and yes even lives lost. The Lord has prompted me to finally share my findings from the Scriptures to inform and exhort others of the dangers of this subtle and very dangerous teaching. This book is dedicated to those who have been hurt. My prayer is that the Lord will speak to the hearts of those who were hurt so that they will be healed, as well as the hearts of those who follow the erroneous teaching, that they will see the errors of this false belief system and help others to be free from this spiritual bondage.

CHAPTER ONE

Sharing Personal Experiences of Spiritual Warfare

Thou therefore gird up thy loins, and arise, and speak unto them all that I command thee: be not dismayed at their faces, lest I confound thee before them. – Jeremiah 1:17

It was October of 1987 in Kansas City, Missouri when I came to know Christ as Savior. I was an active member of the Catholic Church at that time and one night I did something that I had never done before – I opened my Bible. Reading through the Scriptures, I was convicted of my sins and accepted Jesus Christ as my only hope for salvation. That same week I attended a Vineyard church for a wedding and was overwhelmed by all the perceived emotion and excitement. Two weeks later, I left the Catholic Church due to the fact that what was being taught did not align itself to what I was now reading in the Bible.

After many years of what I describe as knowing the face of God yet not knowing the heart of God, I thought I would see for myself what the charismatic church I had recently visited had to offer. I hungered for an exciting experience in church. I had never seen that kind of enthusiasm and emotion in a church.

I would later learn that there was no Biblical substance there, but only emotion and titillation of the senses. We spent about a year and a half there in a futile search to know God better and found it was not a place to be fed with the pure Word of God. There was the praise and worship music, emotions, and my first exposure to demonology. In the Catholic Church, we had heard of exorcisms but had no first hand knowledge nor knew of anyone who did. This was a whole new world for me. At the Vineyard, we heard of territorial demons, ancestral demons, even demons of health, finance, etc. It seemed that around every corner there was a demon. It was even suggested that the wife of one of their self-professed prophets had a distorted facial feature that was attributed to demons.

I felt that I needed to check with the church leadership over this issue as well as other issues over which I was concerned. My only argument as a baby believer was that what I was seeing and hearing did not line up with God's Word. I later learned that these beliefs were based on what I came to know of as "experience based theology". They also used "isogesis" which is the practice of reading things into God's Word rather than "exegesis" which is extracting from what is already written. Isogesis seemed to be the preferred method of Bible study in that church as well as those in the spiritual warfare movement. We left there in search of one that would teach God's Word as written. Our search eventually brought us to an Independent Fundamental Baptist church in Kansas City, Missouri. I felt that of all places, charismatic beliefs would never be found there. I was sorely mistaken.

The first week we were there, the church was holding a seminar. During that seminar, a supernatural story was told. I became quite uncomfortable as it painfully resembled other charismatic teachings in my past.

I immediately stepped out of that meeting and found my pastor and asked him if that type of teaching would be taught in the church. He assured me that it would not, but regrettably that was not the case. That turned out to be the beginning of a very painful experience in the realm of the modern day spiritual warfare movement.

As the years passed I must admit that whenever my pastor taught Scripturally, he was one of the best Bible teachers I had ever met. But the issue at hand was not where the teaching was right, but where it was dangerously wrong. We received a book called "The Bondage Breaker" as well as another book called "Reclaiming Surrendered Ground". In my ignorance as well my unquestioning loyalty to my pastor, I accepted these books. After all, he was well respected in Fundamental circles and who was I to question this teaching. We oftentimes trade discernment for loyalty to our shame.

In 1997, the Lord called me to prepare for the ministry. Before we left for Bible College, I experienced my first spiritual warfare counseling session as it was performed on me.

A few years later, it would be performed on my wife as well. In those sessions, we were told to open ourselves up to allow voices and thoughts to speak through us. It was basically an effort to allow a demon to channel through Christians. We were told to empty our minds. We were asked to identify the name of the demon within us as well as the name of the "gatekeeper".

We were asked when the demon entered and how. We were asked to confess sins. After many questions, the demons were told to leave us. This is ironic as some in the modern day spiritual warfare movement will say that we don't have demons "in" us, but just operating "through" us. So how does a demon leave somewhere he supposedly is not? These sessions and their practices were the norm as I was present in the sessions of others. Fortunately for us while at Bible College, as well as the local church we attended while there, we were fed Scriptural truth and realized that the spiritual warfare teaching was not Biblical. I was hesitant to go against my pastor, but decided I would bite my tongue and accept it as something that perhaps I just didn't quite understand. After all, my pastor had much more experience in the ministry and maybe I just hadn't grasped this area of teaching yet. Regrettably, we all learned the hard way the harm this teaching causes. We were about to see the extent of that harm.

    I was called back to work on staff at my home church and felt that it was a dream come true. On a bright sunny Thursday morning November 2, 2000, most of the staff was present at the daily prayer meeting before classes at the Christian school. Pastor was absent so we went on with the prayer meeting. Several minutes into the meeting the school administrator and the associate pastor were urgently called out. Within a short time we would be told that pastor's wife and daughter were found dead. Our assumption was that they were murdered and that a killer was at large.

    Later we were told that the pastor's wife shot and killed her daughter and turned the gun on herself and committed suicide. We were told that it may have been during a demonic manifestation. It was that week that it was communicated that the pastor's daughter had been demonized and had spoken in guttural tones as well as speaking in the third person. She had been taken to see a spiritual warfare counselor to no avail. We were also told that she was supposedly a victim of a demonic ritual at a very young age and that she had been dedicated to Satan. We were also told that she was a victim of a demonic time-clock which was going off again. It was strongly suggested that the mother was trying to kill the daughter while she was demonically possessed.

But what about being a new creature in Christ - what about old things passing away and all things becoming new? After all, she supposedly had a testimony of salvation.

> *2 Cor. 5:17 "Therefore if any man be in Christ, he is a new creature: old things are passed away; behold, all things are become new."*

> *John 8:36 "If the Son therefore shall make you free, ye shall be free indeed".*

What we saw those first few weeks contradicted the Scriptures in every possible way. While out of loyalty, I wanted to believe the explanation but I could not reconcile it with the Word of God. Other church members were now claiming to see "demonic manifestations" in their spouses. It seemed that this was beginning to snowball. We later spoke to one church member who nearly lost his life due to this truly unbiblical teaching. The following is the personal account of what he was told after fruitless counseling sessions - attempted exorcisms - for what he was experiencing at home.

> "…When I went for counseling, I was told I was the one that had the demon, and if I were somehow able to get rid of the demon, then both my daughters would be free of it also. After trying everything I was told to do, I found it had no effect … At that point, pastor said he did not have an answer for me, and could not help me any further. ***That is when I asked pastor if I were dead, would that solve the problem? His answer was a resounding 'Absolutely!'*** At that

point, I was seriously considering suicide. I was not going to do it to rid myself of the demon. The reason I was going to do it was to free my children from the demon. My thinking was if I were gone, then the demon would be gone too. Also, I was so tired from losing sleep every night – I know I was not thinking correctly. I finally realized that all I ever needed to do was to give it all to the Lord and let HIM take care of it for me. I prayed, "Lord, I cannot do it. Would you do it for me?" From that point on, He brought peace to our home. ***I think people should know why I was going to do the unthinkable***."

Due to all the situations arising I poured myself into the Scriptures to study this out. Regrettably, this is something that should have happened beforehand and not after the fact. But I still thank God for delivering me out of the so-called deliverance ministries.

After hearing of other horrific accounts from other church members and the path that this ministry was taking, I submitted my resignation. I also tried to share with the church leadership what the Lord had shown me through His Word, but they would not listen.

Regrettably over the past 5 years, I have heard many other accounts of churches split, ministries ruined, and the faith of many confounded - all over the modern day spiritual warfare movement. Years ago, I thought that what we went through was the exception rather than the rule. It turns out to be just the opposite. In the following chapters we will look at how the modern day spiritual warfare movement contradicts the Word of God, enslaves believers, deceives un-believers, and other results of this truly unbiblical teaching. We will see how those in the spiritual warfare movement are truly Bondage Makers.

CHAPTER TWO

A Play on Words
Biblical Spiritual Warfare
vs.
Modern Day Spiritual Warfare

"And this I say, lest any man should beguile you with enticing words." Colossians 2:4

The verse used does have its proper context but also has its proper application. Regrettably, based on their actions, most proponents of the modern day spiritual warfare movement do not feel that context is an issue. They manipulate Scripture to defend what they want to believe rather than for what it truly means. They also misuse the application. In Colossians 2:4, we are warned of those who would trap and deceive using artful words. We should take heed of those warnings today when dealing with the modern day spiritual warfare movement.

We will now examine some of the more popular terminology of the Spiritual Warfare movement. Of utmost importance is the term *"warfare"*. This term is found in 2 Corinthians:

> *2 Corinthians 10:3-5 "For though we walk in the flesh, we do not war after the flesh: (For the weapons of our warfare are not carnal, but mighty through God to the pulling down of strong holds;) Casting down imaginations, and every high thing that exalteth itself against the knowledge of God, and bringing into captivity every thought to the obedience of Christ;"*

There is no mention here of casting out demons but imaginations. The emphasis is on the believer acting as a believer should. This behavior, if followed, automatically opposes the devil. It does not speak of taking demons captive or binding them, but taking thoughts captive and binding them.

The Book of Ephesians also speaks regarding this war:

> *Ephesians 10:6-18 "Finally, my brethren, be strong in the Lord, and in the power of his might. Put on the whole armour of God, that ye may be able to stand against the wiles of the devil. For we wrestle not against flesh and blood, but against principalities, against powers, against the rulers of the darkness of this world, against spiritual wickedness in high places. Wherefore take unto you the whole armour of God, that ye may be able to withstand in the evil day, and having done all, to stand. Stand therefore, having your loins girt about with truth, and having on the breastplate of righteousness; And your feet shod with the preparation of the gospel of peace; Above all, taking the shield of faith,*

wherewith ye shall be able to quench all the fiery darts of the wicked. And take the helmet of salvation, and the sword of the Spirit, which is the word of God: Praying always with all prayer and supplication in the Spirit, and watching thereunto with all perseverance and supplication for all saints;"

While this speaks of the wiles of the devil, principalities, powers, rulers of darkness, and spiritual wickedness in high places, it also tells us how to battle in this "spiritual warfare". It does not even hint at anything regarding indwelling demons.

We also must not assume that "principalities and powers" always means demons.

Titus 3:1 "Put them in mind to be subject to principalities and powers, to obey magistrates, to be ready to every good work,"

If we are to make that assumption then are we to believe that Titus 3:1 is instructing us to obey demons? No, neither can we assume that we are always dealing with demons.

Neither of the previous passages speak of the techniques used by today's "Deliverance Ministries" which is another term used by this movement. But is this movement providing deliverance or bondage? Obviously it is the latter. Many in this movement are in bondage as they spend much energy seeking out the demons behind their every problem. They have demons of finance, health, worry, transportation, education, relationships, etc. Basically, if they have things going wrong in their lives and issues that need to be addressed, they can conveniently blame a demon -thus avoiding confronting the reality that God may be either allowing something in their lives or confronting their sins. Are these people truly free in Christ?

This term *"stronghold"* is another common term in the spiritual warfare vocabulary. But just what is a stronghold? The following quote from Barnes Notes clearly defines what it is:

> *"To the pulling down of strong holds. The word here rendered 'stronghold'" ... means, properly, a fastness, fortress, or strong fortification. It is here beautifully used to denote the various obstacles resembling a fortress which exist, and which are designed and adapted to oppose the truth and the triumph of the Christian's cause.*
> *All those obstacles are strongly fortified. The sins of his heart are fortified by long indulgence, and by the hold which they have on his soul."*.[1]

Note the mention of indulgence. This indulgence is something of the will and not imposed by another force. It is a matter of lack of surrender to the Lord. The spiritual warfare camp would have you believe that it is Satan or one of his demons that have control of that stronghold and that you are at their mercy.

They choose to abuse another term in combination with the former called "generational sins". They would have you to believe that a person inherits demons or strongholds from the sins of their parents, grandparents, and beyond. They use a verse, or at least a part of a verse:

> *Exodus 20:5 " ... for I the LORD thy God am a jealous God, visiting the iniquity of the fathers upon the children unto the third and fourth generation...*

It would seem from this passage, if taken out of context, that there are generational sins - or in the case of spiritual warfare - demons which are inherited. But what happens to this teaching when the entire verse is used?

> ***Exodus 20:5-6** " Thou shalt not bow down thyself to them, nor serve them for I the LORD thy God am a jealous God, visiting the iniquity of the fathers upon the children unto the third and fourth generation of them that hate me;*
> *And shewing mercy unto thousands of them that love me, and keep my commandments."*

It seems that these verses in their entirety, as well as contextually, mean something totally different. What the verse *does* say is that those that bowed to other gods have sinned against God, and that there will be an ongoing judgment to those who choose to continue in the same sin just as it was applied to those who practiced it in the past.

It emphasizes that not all the offspring of those who sinned will be judged, but those who "hate" God by practicing the same sin. It seems that it would be hard to find a believer that truly "hates" God. The end of the passage is also frequently left out where it states that God shows mercy to those that love Him and keep His commandments.

It seems quite contrary to God's Word that a child would be condemned for his father's sin - especially in the light that the child mentioned has accepted Christ as Savior. What then do they do with the following passage?

> ***2 Corinthians 5:17** "Therefore if any man be in Christ, he is a new creature: old things are passed away; behold, all things are become new."*

Was the Holy Spirit trying to tell us that the caveat to 2 Corinthians 5:17 was Exodus 20:5-6? No, but quite the contrary, as these verses are in full agreement as all Scripture is with itself.

Another point in the area of generational sins is their usage of Adam's sin as an example. They say that since we inherited Adam's sin, it is thus feasible that we can inherit other sins or be in bondage to them.

Romans 5:12 "Wherefore, as by one man sin entered into the world, and death by sin; and so death passed upon all men, for that all have sinned:"

Once again they claim a verse to attempt to justify their views that contextually has nothing to do with the modern day version of spiritual warfare. If one were to embrace this in the sense of spiritual warfare, then one must carry this thought out to its logical conclusion and be able to be delivered from this with spiritual warfare. We have indeed been delivered from the spiritual death that passed unto all men but not through modern day spiritual warfare.

Romans 5:19 "For as by one man's disobedience many were made sinners, so by the obedience of one shall many be made righteous."

This came by obedience in accepting the sacrifice of Christ at the cross, and thus we are made righteous. We still have a sin nature, but that has nothing to do with their version of generational sins or of the Biblical context found within the verses of Exodus 20.

While there is endless terminology used as well as abused by those in the "Deliverance Ministries", the greatest danger lies in the subtlety of those uses. They attempt to sugarcoat their terms in an effort to make them more palatable to more Fundamentally sound churches. They use window dressing and as the chapter is titled "a play on words". But why do they need to play with words? Would not the actual meanings suffice?

The answer lies in that while the truth sets some free it condemns others in their errors. While an error is an error, two errors seem to stand out among the rest. The use of the terms *"oppression"* and *"possession"* travel even beyond the boundaries of error. Those in the "deliverance ministries" would be the first to say that a born again believer cannot be possessed but oppressed. At the surface, it sounds acceptable and opens doors into churches that would otherwise be unreceptive to this unbiblical concept of spiritual warfare. The issue is in that their definition of "oppressed" matches the Biblical definition of "possessed" - which is an impossibility for a believer.

One clear error on their part is their claim that a believer can be "severely oppressed by demons."[2] Not that a believer can't be severely oppressed in a Biblical manner, but just what do they mean by severely oppressed? One example in Chapter 3 of "The Bondage Breaker" and another in the introduction of the same book are two stories which are related regarding a woman who is supposedly a believer and has a demon, or as Anderson states "the evil one"[3] speaking through her. Or of the woman who said "I've been scratching myself like this, and I can't control it…"[4] (The entire quote will not be printed here as God's Word tells us to be innocent concerning evil things.)

Romans 16:19b "… but yet I would have you wise unto that which is good, and simple concerning evil."

It seems that this is an area that they choose to ignore and instead prefer to defile others with vile accounts in their books. They prefer sensational stories while dragging the minds of Christians through the world's gutters. But the examples previously stated do not sound like someone who is Biblically "severely oppressed", but of one who is Biblically possessed. Note the following verses and their stunning resemblances to their examples.

> *Mark 5:1-15 "And they came over unto the other side of the sea, into the country of the Gadarenes. And when he was come out of the ship, immediately there met him out of the tombs a man with an unclean spirit, ...And always, night and day, he was in the mountains, and in the tombs, crying, and <u>cutting himself</u> with stones. ...<u>And cried with a loud voice, and said, What have I to do with thee, Jesus, thou Son of the most high God? I adjure thee by God</u>, that thou torment me not. For he said unto him, Come out of the man, thou unclean spirit. And he asked him, What is thy name? And he answered, saying, My name is Legion: for we are many. ... And they that fed the swine fled, and told it in the city, and in the country. And they went out to see what it was that was done. And they come to Jesus, and see him that was <u>possessed with the devil</u> , and had the legion, sitting, and clothed, and in his right mind: and they were afraid."*

Another claim is of the return of demons that are cast out. An important point of note is that there is never any mention of the demons returning once cast out in the Scriptures. They claim the following verse once again out of context:

> *Matthew 12:43-45 "When the unclean spirit is gone out of a man, he walketh through dry places, seeking rest, and findeth none. Then he saith, I will return into my house from whence I came out; and*

when he is come, he findeth it empty, swept, and garnished. Then goeth he, and taketh with himself seven other spirits more wicked than himself, and they enter in and dwell there: and the last state of that man is worse than the first. Even so shall it be also unto this wicked generation."

Is the verse quoted a viable proof text for the belief that demons can return? The answer is absolutely not based on the following proofs.

First and foremost the context must be addressed. It is very well expressed by Albert Barnes:

> "The general sentiment which our Saviour here teaches is much more easily understood than the illustration which he uses. The Jews had asked a sign from heaven that should decisively prove that he was the Messiah, and satisfy their unbelief. He replies, that though he should give them such a sign—a proof conclusive and satisfactory; and though for a time they should **profess** to believe, and **apparently reform** yet such was the **obstinacy of their unbelief and wickedness**, that they would soon return to them, and become worse and worse. Infidelity and wickedness, like an evil spirit in a possessed man, were appropriately at home in them. If driven out, **they would find no other place so comfortable and undisturbed** as their bosoms. Everywhere they would be comparatively like an evil spirit going through deserts and lonely places, and finding no place of rest. They would return, therefore, and dwell with them."[5] (emphasis mine)

What is addressed in this verse regarding demonology actually supports the fact that those to whom a demon did return were never converted in the first place. The born again believer does not merely *profess* to believe but *truly* believes. There is no *apparent* reform, but *true* reform. There is no unbelief in their belief on their Savior. Theirs is a place that would no longer be comfortable for a demon due to the presence of the Holy Spirit of God.

As the quote stated, the true context in the verses (which started at verse 38 of Matthew 12) was about the scribes and Pharisees seeking a sign and not about demonology.

But what of the word used in Mark, chapter 5 for possessed? The Greek word used here is "daimonizomai". This word as described by Barnes is stated thus as:

> "In the NT, these are persons, afflicted with especially severe diseases, either bodily or mentally, (such as paralysis, blindness, deafness, loss of speech, epilepsy, melancholy, insanity, etc.) whose bodies in the opinion of the Jews demons had entered, and <u>so held possession of them as not only to afflict them with ills, but also to dethrone the reason and take its place themselves; accordingly the possessed were wont to express the mind and consciousness of the demons dwelling in them</u>(emphasis mine); and their cure was thought to require the expulsion of the demon."[6]

The word expulsion means that an entity is somewhere and needs to be removed. So is a demon being expulsed? From a believer?

It would seem that those who are referred to today by the spiritual warfare camp as oppressed would qualify to be Biblically possessed.

Attention should be paid to the fact that those referred to in the Scriptures were not said to be believers, as well as the fact that there was no permanent indwelling of the

Holy Spirit had they been so. The fact that a believer cannot be Biblically possessed or severely oppressed according to their terms will be shown in the following chapter.

The only viable explanation would be that those in Anderson's examples were either spiritually lost, mentally unstable, deceived by the spiritual warfare movement, or frauds. Here also lies a two-fold error in terms of mental illness. In the book "The Bondage Breaker", in a section titled "Common Misconceptions About Bondage", two statements are made in an attempt to validate these viewpoints. One statement claimed to be a misconception is that "What the early church called demonic activity we now understand to be mental illness"[7] and the other is "Some problems are psychological and some are spiritual"[8]. Are these truly misconceptions?

They would have us to believe that if these mental illnesses cannot be proven to be physical they then must be assumed to be spiritual. But it seems that God's Word would not be in agreement with their conclusions.

Matthew 4:24 "And his fame went throughout all Syria: and they brought unto him all sick people that were taken with divers diseases and torments, and those which were possessed with devils, and those which were lunatick, and those that had the palsy; and he healed them."

It seems that the Scriptures differentiate diseases and torments from those possessed with devils as well as from those who were "lunatick" and those that had the palsy.

Mark 1:32-34 "And at even, when the sun did set, they brought unto him all that were diseased, and them that were possessed with devils. And all the city was gathered together at the door. And he healed many that were sick of divers diseases, and cast out many devils; and suffered not the devils to speak, because they knew him."

Notice that some were healed of "divers diseases" while others had devils cast out. These were two separate circumstances.

That is not to say that there were not instances in the Scriptures where some had a genuine disease as well as being demon possessed, but they were recognized and dealt with hand in hand. It was not that the man mentioned in the following verse was "dumb", therefore the demon was cast out so he could speak, but that he was demon possessed and dumb. It cannot be assumed that all those who were healed of diseases were demon possessed especially since this is not found in God's Word.

But note should be made regarding the Biblical examples used by the spiritual warfare movement. In using those verses to defend spiritual warfare, they need to recognize that none of those people had an indwelling Holy Spirit as well as the fact that a permanent indwelling Holy Spirit was not available until the Day of Pentecost. It seems that dispensationalism is ignored by those in the spiritual warfare movement.

It is obvious that the words used as well as the context are critical to what is being communicated. If we are to ignore these basics as well as dispensational principles, then anyone could claim anything to be true. One would then become one's own authority rather than God's Word being that authority.

Another term used is the ***"spiritual warfare counselor"*** which is their term for an ***"exorcist"***. This "counselor" or "specialist" is able to do for the oppressed what God's Word and the pastor seem unable to do. The counselor does not "counsel" but attempts to "channel" as well as do war with Satan and his demons toe to toe.

Apparently the following words no longer apply to the spiritual warfare camp.

> *James 4:7 Submit yourselves therefore to God. Resist the devil, and he will flee from you.*

The word "resist" is in the active voice and not the passive, thus stating that it is an act done by the one whom the devil must flee from and not by the "counselor". Again Albert Barnes correctly states:

> "While you yield to God in all things, you are to yield to the devil in none. You are to resist and oppose him in whatever way he may approach you, whether by allurements, by flattering promises, by the fascinations of the world, by temptation, or by threats."[9]

Note that the commentator does not mention indwelling demons. Several questions arise that must be answered. Why weren't the early Christians made aware of these necessary "techniques" such as channeling with demons through Christians, burning inanimate objects, binding and casting demons out of Christians and so on? There is no record of it in the early church. How then has the church survived for over 2000 years without the need for the modern day spiritual warfare movement? The answer is quite simple. Man created modern day spiritual warfare and man also created the supposed need. This supposed need will be addressed in a later chapter.

"Memory recollection" is another term that must be discussed as this is one of the more radical beliefs taught in spiritual warfare. They teach that before you can be "deliv-

ered" from a "stronghold" or demon you must be able to remember where you supposedly allowed that "spirit" to enter. They say that you must be able to identify the date in order to deal with it, and thus "send an eviction notice"[10] to the demon, or in other words exorcise the demon.

They conveniently say that if you cannot "recollect" with God's help the entry point, it must be an inherited demon - thus they have their bases covered against critics. There have been claims of recollections of "entry points" at ages where one could not even understand what was going on. It seems that they always have their safety valve as was in the case of memory recollection.

They argue that those who oppose them or their teaching are working for the "enemy" and are themselves oppressed. But one interesting note is that they themselves claim that if a person is "unapproachable," it is a sign of the stronghold of pride and needs to be dealt with. It is ironic that many of the proponents of the spiritual warfare movement are very unapproachable when confronted with the Scriptures that oppose their way of thinking. Would that mean that they have a stronghold?

There are endless terms within the modern day spiritual warfare movement such as generational sins, bondage, ownership, demonic time-clocks (a demonic time bomb of sorts where the demons come by at a pre-programmed time), deliverance, oppression, possession, influence, curses, religious strongholds, sexual strongholds, strongholds of many kinds, carriers (people, animals, toys, videos, and even given names), and too many others to be named or discussed in this short chapter, most of which are not found in God's Word. Those that are found in God's Word carry much different meanings than that used in their movement. Needless to say, books could be written solely addressing the words they use and how those words are manipulated.

The issue is to follow the Word of God and to let that be the sole authority. Not to seek words to justify what we wish to believe, but to allow God's Word to determine what we believe. Not based on our experiences and preconceived notions, but based on Biblical history as God has communicated it. The spiritual warfare movement far too often attempts to use their understanding of the world and thus make assumptions of the spiritual.

A perfect example is as follows as Steve Curington of Reformers Unanimous claims:

> "Powers means authorities. Reporting directly to the devil in his chain of command are an array of authorities who oversee the work of his evil minions. Rulers is simply another word for leaders. Underneath the first level of demonic authorities is a huge contingent of leadership. For someone to be a leader, they must have followers.
>
> Using 'the world's' corporate chain of command system that we know from the workplace for an example, we can assume the level one phase of leadership has a minimum of two subordinates, called powers. Each power at this level of authority would have at least two rulers (leaders under him). These rulers would have at least seven followers that would be in subjection to them in the chain of command. Thus it is quite possible that any individual on earth could face up to 33 demonic forces working against them! That's why we tell our students that 'new levels bring new devils'.
>
> I guess with this many delegates under his authority, it's no wonder that the devil only became personally involved in the temptation of Eve, Job, and Jesus. Everyone else he has delegated to his huge chain of command."[11]

Now take note of the words that were used in the above quote. From where does he **Biblically** derive his figure of "33 demonic forces"? He said "using the world's corporate chain of command system", "we know from the workplace", "we can assume", "it is quite possible", and "I guess". It seems that there is an enormous amount of guessing as well as rationalization using man's understanding and no support from the Scriptures to prove his claims. Their guide to spiritual warfare should not be a Fortune 500 company, nor demons through channeling, but God's Word.

Note should be made that Mr. Curington does correctly acknowledge that a believer cannot be internally influenced by a demon, although issue can be taken in inferences to demons being responsible for more than need be. The point here is that we cannot make assumptions which will only cause spiritual confusion. The guide for the Christian must be God's Word and not modern day movements.

This brings us to another term called "addiction". It seems that we have embraced the world in attempting to identify everything with a sickness or disease. The term "addiction" has been coupled with "oppression". These words have been intertwined in order to promote another version of spiritual warfare as well as in the weakening of the church. This relationship will be addressed later. But using words such as addictions to alcohol, drugs, pornography, eating, and credit would be better served with Biblical terms so they can be addressed in a Biblical manner. The Bible refers to the alcoholic as a drunk who is in sin. The so-called addictions to alcohol, sex, drugs, pornography, eating, credit cards, and whatever terms they choose to use, fall under the classification of the lust of the flesh, lust of the eyes, and the pride of life - all of which are sin.

There is an answer to all these problems. That answer is called salvation and death to self. Yes, there are outside influences such as demonic forces, but there are also other things called the world and the flesh.

It seems that those in this movement want us to focus on demons, thereby falling into a true trap of the devil. When we begin to play with God's Word we begin to play with our faith. There can be nothing more dangerous that that.

CHAPTER THREE

Who Can and Who Cannot be "Demonized"

Acts 20:28 "Take heed therefore unto yourselves, and to all the flock, over the which the Holy Ghost hath made you overseers, to feed the church of God, which <u>he hath purchased</u> with his own blood."

As it has been previously stated, a born- again blood bought believer cannot be demon possessed because he is God possessed. (Keep in mind that what the spiritual warfare movement calls demonized or oppressed indeed means to be Biblically possessed.) This is not to say that demonic possession is an impossibility, but that it is an impossibility for a born again believer. Acts 20:28 tells us that we have been "purchased" by God with the blood of Christ.

There is also another issue and that is one of location truths regarding God and Satan. The spiritual warfare movement chooses to play with the words "giving place to the devil" as well as "demons in Christians" in a topographical sense. But what then of the following verse?

> *I John 4:4 "Ye are of God, little children, and have overcome them: because greater is he that is in you, than he that is in the world."*

Since they choose to dwell on "topography"[12] as they state it, then the previous verse speaks volumes regarding topography. The verse states that there are two entities located in two different locations. One is <u>**God**</u> who dwells <u>*in the believer*</u> while the other is the <u>***Devil***</u> which dwells <u>*in the world*</u>. They should not use the Scriptures in an attempt to justify their beliefs and ignore the same Scriptures when it is not convenient to their purposes.

> *II Corinthians 6:14 " Be ye not unequally yoked together with unbelievers: for what fellowship hath righteousness with unrighteousness? and what communion hath light with darkness?"*

> *Ephesians 5:8 "For ye were sometimes darkness, but now are ye light in the Lord: walk as children of light:"*

The Bible is very clear regarding the fact that we were in darkness and are now in the Light. Darkness and light are two very opposite locations which cannot co-exist because they are opposites. The following verse speaks of the fact that demons could not even stand to be in the presence of God.

> *Mark 1:24 "Saying, Let us alone; what have we to do with thee, thou Jesus of Nazareth? art thou*

come to destroy us? I know thee who thou art, the Holy One of God."

Is this not the same God which dwells in every believer?

I Corinthians 6:19 What? know ye not that your body is the temple of the Holy Ghost <u>which is in you</u>, which ye have of God, and ye are not your own?"

Are they then willing to say that they no longer believe in the indwelling Holy Spirit of God? Will they now deny the Trinity? I Cor. 6:19 tells us that we have an indwelling Holy Spirit of God. Are they implying that a demon is now cohabitating with the Holy Spirit of God within the temple of God? Are they saying that a demon no longer has a problem being in the presence of God's Holy Spirit? And what of the permanence of the Holy Spirit? And what of the security of the believer? Is it only for salvation or is it not for more?

John 16:13 " Howbeit when he, the Spirit of truth, is come, he will guide you into all truth: for he shall not speak of himself; but whatsoever he shall hear, that shall he speak: and he will shew you things to come."

Ephesians 4:30 "And grieve not the holy Spirit of God, whereby <u>ye are sealed</u> unto the day of redemption."

While a believer can grieve the Holy Spirit and thus yield less of his life to the Holy Spirit, there is no mention in the Bible that we have differing measures of the Holy Spirit's presence in our lives.

But what happens when a former lost person first trusts Christ as Savior?

> *I Peter 1:23 "Being born again, not of corruptible seed, but of incorruptible, by the word of God, which liveth and abideth for ever."*

To begin with, as is stated in I Peter as well as John chapter 3, man was born again. But were we saved from our sins only to be in bondage to demons until we get to heaven?

> *John 8:36 If the Son therefore shall make you free, ye shall be free indeed.*

Based on the previous verse, we were set free. We were set free from the bondage and dominion of sin. We are no longer under the old master, but under the new.

> *Romans 6:22 But now being made free from sin, and become servants to God, ye have your fruit unto holiness, and the end everlasting life.*

There is not one mention in the Scriptures of a born again believer being demonically oppressed as described by the spiritual warfare movement. There is not one instance of a born again believer having spiritual warfare conducted on him. There is not even mention of a spiritual warfare counselor. The following are the most common examples used by the spiritual warfare movement of demonized believers as well as the arguments against the using of those examples.

Peter

The use of Peter by the spiritual warfare movement is one of the most widely used as well as the most erroneous. The following verse is used as their proof text:

Matthew 16:23 "But he turned, and said unto Peter, Get thee behind me, Satan: thou art an offence unto me: for thou savourest not the things that be of God, but those that be of men."

They would have you to believe that it was Satan taking control over Peter and speaking through him or as they would say "demonic oppression". They also believe that the Lord was rebuking Satan as an entity within Peter. But based on a literal interpretation of this passage, just the opposite is communicated. But to further examine this issue, let us review the verses before and after that incident as well as those speaking of the incident directly.

Mark 16:15-24 "He saith unto them, But whom say ye that I am? And Simon Peter answered and said, Thou art the Christ, the Son of the living God. And Jesus answered and said unto him, Blessed art thou, Simon Barjona: for flesh and blood hath not revealed it unto thee, but my Father which is in heaven. And I say also unto thee, That thou art Peter, and upon this rock I will build my church; and the gates of hell shall not prevail against it. And I will give unto thee the keys of the kingdom of heaven: and whatsoever thou shalt bind on earth shall be bound in heaven: and whatsoever thou shalt loose on earth shall be loosed in heaven. Then charged he his disciples that they should tell no man that he was Jesus the Christ. From that time forth began Jesus to shew unto his disciples, how that he must go unto Jerusalem, and suffer many things of the elders and chief priests and scribes, and be killed, and be raised again the third day. Then Peter took him, and began to rebuke him, saying, Be it far from thee, Lord: this shall not be unto thee. But he turned, and said unto Peter, Get thee behind me, Satan: thou art an offence unto me: for thou savourest not the things that be of God, but those that be of men. Then said Jesus unto his disciples, If any man will come after me, let him deny himself, and take up his cross, and follow me."

In verses 15-17, this supposed satanically influenced man has just been used by God to proclaim a truth. They may argue that under other circumstances demons declared Christ's identity. But in those cases those demons were addressed as such. In these verses, Peter is referred to as Simon Barjona and not Satan. Was there then a metamorphosis that took place? Of course not! But then how does one explain verses 22-23?

One obvious oversight on the part of the spiritual warfare movement is addressed in verse 22 which states that "Peter took him, and began to rebuke him." It was not Satan, nor a demon, it was none other than Peter according to God's Word.

Would it not also have been odd for Satan to call Jesus "Lord" in this verse if it indeed was Satan speaking to Jesus rather than Peter?

In Matthew Chapter 4 during the temptation in the wilderness, Satan does not address Jesus as "Lord". Why would he now?

But what of the Lord's rebuke? In verse 23 we read "But he turned, and said unto Peter, Get thee behind me, Satan." The Bible is quite clear that he was addressing Peter and not Satan as we read "said to Peter". In all other cases He addressed the demons directly even asking their names. Would He not have addressed Satan had He been rebuking Satan? If Peter was truly demonically influenced why then did the Lord not bind Satan and cast him out thus freeing Peter? This conversation comes to its logical conclusion in verses 24-26 when it speaks of the necessary sacrifices involved which even included potential loss of life. Was the Lord trying to teach Satan about sacrifice? No, He was teaching Peter and the others about the cost of true sacrifice for God. He was only making a comparison of Peter's selfishness with that of Satan's.

This leads us to the obvious that this verse has no place in the argument for spiritual warfare.

Ananias and Sapphira

The use of verses which contain Ananias and Sapphira as a proof text for spiritual warfare contain many questions which must be addressed.

We accept the fact that Ananias and Sapphira were members of the first century church and that many at that time gave their possessions for the cause of Christ unlike the selfish action of Ananias and Sapphira. But were they demon oppressed or controlled because of their choice?

> ***Acts 5:1-11 "But a certain man named Ananias, with Sapphira his wife, sold a possession, And kept back part of the price, his wife also being privy to it, and brought a certain part, and laid it at the apostles' feet. But Peter said, Ananias, why hath Satan filled thine heart to lie to the Holy Ghost, and to keep back part of the price of the land? Whiles it remained, was it not thine own? and after it was sold, was it not in thine own power? why hast thou***

conceived this thing in thine heart? thou hast not lied unto men, but unto God. And Ananias hearing these words fell down, and gave up the ghost: and great fear came on all them that heard these things. And the young men arose, wound him up, and carried him out, and buried him. And it was about the space of three hours after, when his wife, not knowing what was done, came in. And Peter answered unto her, Tell me whether ye sold the land for so much? And she said, Yea, for so much. Then Peter said unto her, How is it that ye have agreed together to tempt the Spirit of the Lord? behold, the feet of them which have buried thy husband are at the door, and shall carry thee out. Then fell she down straightway at his feet, and yielded up the ghost: and the young men came in, and found her dead, and, carrying her forth, buried her by her husband. And great fear came upon all the church, and upon as many as heard these things."

The first issue to be addressed is the assumption that they were demonized. That thought is not stated anywhere in this passage or in any other for that matter. What *is* stated is that Peter is addressing Ananias and not a demon. While Peter does state "why hath Satan filled thine heart," he is dealing with Ananias' choice of submitting to a temptation - a choice which goes back to the garden. As was the case in the Garden of Eden with Adam and Eve, temptation was placed before him as well and he had a free will choice to either submit to it or reject it. In both cases, both parties chose to submit to temptation. Barnes states:

"The sin of Ananias consisted in his yielding to the temptation. Nowhere in the Bible are men supposed to be free from guilt, from the fact that they have been tempted to commit it. God requires them to resist temptation; and if they yield to it, they must be punished."[13]

The only thing that can be derived from Peter's statement to Ananias is that he was confronting Ananias' free will choice to deceive. Peter states to Ananias "why hast thou conceived this thing in thine heart?" The verb conceived is in the middle voice indicating an action that has been performed by Ananias and was not conceived by another source such as a demon. Sapphira as well is confronted in much the same manner and they both meet the same fate. This fate was not because of so -called spiritual warfare, but was a result of lying to the Holy Spirit.

This episode is meant to teach us as well as to leave an example to the first century church of the dangers of hypocrisy as well the need of keeping the church pure. If this were indeed an issue of demonization, then why did Peter not bind and cast out the demons within Ananias and Sapphira? Why did he not address the demons? Why did he not free them from "spiritual bondage" due to their oppression? Why did he not use the techniques used by the so-called modern day spiritual warfare movement? Why did he not attempt to channel the demons' voices through them?

The reason is because they were not demonized and there is no Biblical proof that they were. Once again the spiritual warfare movement has taken a verse out of its context in an attempt to justify their beliefs.

King David and the Numbering of the People

It seems impossible that one would attempt to use the following as a proof text for spiritual warfare, especially keeping in mind the dispensational differences. Even the very context does not lend itself to spiritual warfare. But as is usually the case, context is forsaken.

> **I Chronicles 21:1 "And Satan stood up against Israel, and provoked David to number Israel."**

On the surface one would question if perhaps the spiritual warfare proponents have a verse they can finally use. One must look at the word "provoked" which means "to entice" which we would interpret today as temptation. But besides its contextual and literal interpretation, there are other arguments. One thing the spiritual warfare movement has seemed to overlook is that this is the same story as told in II Samuel 24.

Whether their oversight was intentional or not would be purely speculation. I and II Chronicles are basically repetitions of the Books I and II Samuel as well as I and II Kings, thus they would need to agree contextually although written at a different time. It seems ironic that they chose to use the recount found in I Chronicles 21:1 rather than the account in II Samuel 24:1. But II Samuel states it in a clearer sense, albeit inconvenient to the spiritual warfare cause.

> **II Samuel 24:1 "And again the anger of the LORD was kindled against Israel, and he moved David against them to say, Go, number Israel and Judah."**

If one were to now take both II Samuel 24:1 along with I Chronicles 21:1, one would see that this verse could not be used for an argument in favor of spiritual warfare.

Based on the account given within the two verses, a simple conclusion would stand out. This conclusion would be that "Satan stood up against Israel" as well as "provoked David" based upon "the anger of the LORD was kindled against Israel" as well as "he (being God) moved David against them to say, Go, number Israel and Judah." This would line up well with the precedence set in Job 1:8, as well as Job 2:3, where we read, "And the LORD said unto Satan, Hast thou considered my servant Job". A perfect explanation is found in the Jamieson, Fausset, Brown Commentary:

> "God, though He cannot tempt any man (#Jas 1:13), is frequently described in Scripture as doing what He merely permits to be done; and so, in this case, He permitted Satan to tempt David. ..."[14]

Thus once again those defending spiritual warfare with the previously mentioned verses cannot support them contextually.

It is quite evident that a Christian cannot be demonically oppressed as they define it. This conclusion is reached based on the Word of God in its context. There is no precedence set forth in the Bible nor in early church history or even in recent church history to support this (excluding recent Charismatic teachings which are known to be doctrinally in error). This leads us now to who can be possessed.

The Unbeliever

In every instance of demonic possession in the Scriptures, those possessed were lost men and women. This leads to one of the most dangerous aspects of the teaching of modern day spiritual warfare. Is the counselee indeed a believer? Or is he an unbeliever that thinks he is a Christian? Is the spiritual warfare counselor deceiving a lost person into getting "treatment" for something that a believer cannot have? This leaves the counselee in his lost state thinking that he is saved, while in reality he is condemned to hell.

It is the belief of many that a large number of people who consider themselves to be Christians are indeed lost people. This would not only explain why some of these counselees truly are manifesting strange things in their lives, but also would explain much regarding the lack of change in the lives of many who profess to be Christians. This is not a blanket statement regarding people who exhibit slow or little spiritual growth, but it should cause some to question their salvation.

If they are believers, they would be as previously stated: either deceived, deceivers, or mentally unstable. We are also in an age of easy believism with our "be what you want to be" and "do what you want to do" mentality. Today's church is having very little if any real impact on the world. Is that possibly because many of these "church members" are lost? We constantly meet people who think they are Christians because they attend church, give faithfully, or have relatives who have been members of churches for long periods of time. But being in a church makes one a Christian as much as standing in a parking lot makes one a car. The Bible is quite clear regarding our new life in Christ. One must be born-again! So then the question must be seriously posed: are these counselees saved to begin with?

What can and what cannot be demonized?

The subject of many horror movies has been a portrayal of an inanimate object that is controlled by a spirit and runs rampant causing havoc everywhere it goes. It does cause one to wonder why the many stories that are communicated regarding demonization bare such a striking resemblance to old horror movies. Is the Christian life now imitating so-called art?

The teachers within the spiritual warfare movement would have you to believe that there are many examples of animals as well as inanimate objects possessed by demons.

But let us examine their claims. There are two Biblical examples of animals being possessed in the same sense as man being possessed. They would cite the example of the demoniacs of Gadara.

> *Matthew 8: 30-32 " And there was a good way off from them an herd of many swine feeding. So the devils besought him, saying, If thou cast us out, suffer us to go away into the herd of swine. And he said unto them, Go. And when they were come out, they went into the herd of swine: and, behold, the whole herd of swine ran violently down a steep place into the sea, and perished in the waters."*

But did the demons possess these swine out of regular habit or out of a choice in facing banishment?

> *Mark 5:10-13 "And he besought him much that he would not send them away out of the country. Now there was there nigh unto the mountains a great herd of swine feeding. And all the devils besought him, saying, Send us into the swine, that we may enter into them. And forthwith Jesus gave them leave. And the unclean spirits went out, and entered into the swine: and the herd ran violently down a steep place into the sea, (they were about two thousand;) and were choked in the sea."*

There are no other examples of demons within animals other than Satan in the garden. But they claim that this is a standard within that realm.

But what of inanimate objects? They would have you to believe that by the Christian possessing certain objects (even out of ignorance), demonic forces can be transported into their lives. 'They claim an example of a young boy who was innocently watching a certain cartoon (albeit a poor one for a Christian family to watch) and became demonically possessed. He had to have a demon cast out by a spiritual warfare counselor because demons were transported via the cartoon'.[15] They claim that this is not the exception, but the rule. But where is the Biblical precedence for this?

Their claim is that certain objects are dedicated to demons and thus become carriers of demons. If this is the case then Satanists and others could go to Wal-Mart and dedicate everything to Satan thus sending legions of demons into the homes of Christians. While this all sounds ridiculous, it is being embraced by many in our Fundamental circles.

Why is this being accepted? Simply because we are not consulting the Word of God.

This is not to say that Christians should not stay away from certain things that can spiritually harm us in a Biblical way. We actually should discern carefully what we watch, where we go, what we say, how we think, and all these things should be dictated by God's Word.

I Corinthians 10:31 Whether therefore ye eat, or drink, or whatsoever ye do, do all to the glory of God.

II Corinthians 6:14-7:1 "Be ye not unequally yoked together with unbelievers: for what fellowship hath righteousness with unrighteousness? and what communion hath light with darkness? And what concord hath Christ with Belial? or what part hath he that believeth with an infidel? And what agreement hath the temple of God with idols? for ye are the temple of the living God; as God hath said, I will dwell in them, and walk in them; and I will be their God, and they shall be my people. Wherefore come out from among them, and be ye separate, saith the Lord, and touch not the unclean thing; and I will receive you, And will be a Father unto you, and ye shall be my sons and daughters, saith the Lord Almighty. Having therefore these promises, dearly beloved, let us cleanse ourselves from all filthiness of the flesh and spirit, perfecting holiness in the fear of God."

In summary, it has been Scripturally shown that a born again believer cannot be demonized as described by the spiritual warfare movement. It is also clear that the ownership of inanimate objects by believers is not an open door for demonization. And finally there is no Biblical precedence for demonic possession of animals. It would seem that the only true candidate for demonization would be a lost person in need of salvation.

CHAPTER FOUR

The Devil Made Me Do It

James1:12-15 "Blessed is the man that endureth temptation: for when he is tried, he shall receive the crown of life, which the Lord hath promised to them that love him. Let no man say when he is tempted, I am tempted of God: for God cannot be tempted with evil, neither tempteth he any man: But every man is tempted, when he is drawn away of his own lust, and enticed. Then when lust hath conceived, it bringeth forth sin: and sin, when it is finished, bringeth forth death."

In the early 1970's a secular comedian made the phrase "the devil made me do it" popular.

"...For his opening monologue in that special, Wilson told a story about a minister's wife who tried to justify her new extravagant purchase by explaining how 'the Devil made me buy this dress!'..."[16]

Millions of lost television viewers would roar with laughter at the use of that phrase based on how ridiculous it was that the character was trying to use the devil as his scapegoat for his irresponsible actions.

But what even the secular world was able to discern as impossible, some in the church are embracing as doctrine. But was the comedian's intention in his joke very different from the intentions or desires of some who practice spiritual warfare? After all it is quite convenient to be able to sin away your life blaming it on the "devil" so there is no accountability for your actions. It actually resembles the Catholic confessional in some ways - to be able to sin and erase, sin and erase, and live your life on a spiritual rollercoaster. But does this pattern line up with the Bible?

> **Romans 6:15 What then? shall we sin, because we are not under the law, but under grace? God forbid.**

One example is of a church in North Carolina that has a so-called "Deliverance Ministry". The stories are endless of people participating in immorality, drinking, drugs, gossip, etc. all week and then appearing at the altar on Sunday to have the demons supposedly cast out, only to repeat the cycle on Monday. After all isn't this very convenient?

Isn't this in essence what is being taught by those in the spiritual warfare movement? According to them, it obviously isn't their fault they are sinning. Perhaps they watched the wrong cartoon when they were young. Perhaps their great-grandparents dabbled in witchcraft. Perhaps they bought a toy at a garage sale that was dedicated to Satan. They may have cast out the demons only to have them return when they said "We're back!" (this is a supposed quote from a "demon" during an encounter and coincidentally is also a quote from another horror movie). It could have been a "sleeper" demon hiding out. It might have even been one that came in when they were too young to know it, their power of recollection failed them, and thus they are tormented. Or worst of all they didn't know of modern day spiritual warfare (because it can not be found in the Scriptures) and they are condemned for that. But through all this, according to the spiritual warfare movement, some of these people are only victims.

> "In this case Lydia is portrayed as a victim. Here is a poor Christian, indwelt, possessed, and controlled by a demon. She is not to blame for her foul language or her abusive speech..." According to Anderson she is a "poor victim, with damaged self esteem, indwelt by a demon,"[17]

It seems that the spiritual warfare movement is getting its doctrine from afternoon talk shows rather than God's Word. The church today needs to get back to making God's Word the standard for understanding what is and what is not going on around us.

But sadly it is not just the talk shows which have a distorted view of the responsibility of sin. We also see this within the church. Here Steve Curington of Reformers Unanimous states:

> "So many times as I've dealt with men and women who are struggling with their addiction, I've heard them twist the Word of God to try to justify something they want to do. What causes that? Oppression —outside pressure from the enemy that is trying to get control of their souls."[18]

Romans 7:22-35 "For I delight in the law of God after the inward man: But I see another law in my members, warring against the law of my mind, and

bringing me into captivity to the law of sin which is in my members. O wretched man that I am! who shall deliver me from the body of this death? I thank God through Jesus Christ our Lord. So then with the mind I myself serve the law of God; but with the flesh the law of sin."

But where is the oppression in this verse? Where are the demons? Paul doesn't seem to seek excuses or programs. Again Mr. Curington states:

"If God does not give us the spirit of fear, then pray tell, by process of elimination, who is it from? It's from the devil. An evil spirit that causes you to be apprehensive and concerned is caused by outside pressure."[19]

"If God is not in control of your life, and you seize the authority from Him, it does not mean that you are in control. Rather, you are out of control- under the influence of the devil."[20]

While the quotes mentioned contain some truth, they are also open ended statements that could imply once again that the world and the flesh have no part in influencing the believer for wrong. The truth is that the devil cannot make you do anything! Everyone is responsible for their own actions. There are influences both positive as well as negative in everyone's lives, but the ultimate choice is yours.

Joshua 24:15 "And if it seem evil unto you to serve the LORD, choose you this day whom ye will serve; whether the gods which your fathers served that were on the other side of the flood, or the gods of the Amorites, in whose land ye dwell: but as for me and my house, we will serve the LORD."

The devil didn't make you do it!

CHAPTER FIVE

An Epidemic and The Real Enemy

I Timothy 1:4 "Neither give heed to fables and endless genealogies, which minister questions, rather than godly edifying which is in faith: so do."

If someone desired to break into a home that had a watchdog barring the entrance, he would have to find a way to get the dog away from the door. The thief would simply need to throw a bone away from the door and while the dog went after the bone the thief could spoil the home. It seems that Satan has found the perfect way to distract Christians from their true work. He has tossed the bone of spiritual warfare and the church has left its post in order to get the bone. It is not unlike the dog which chased his tail only to regret catching it in the end. This painful result will be discussed in the last chapter.

The unbiblical spiritual warfare movement has become an epidemic, an enslaver and a seller of fables. It is no longer satisfied to reside in Pentecostal churches, but has invaded Fundamental churches. It is seen in seminars, books, Bible colleges, self improvement programs, etc. While they claim that they don't believe that there is a demon around every corner, there seems to be modern day spiritual warfare around every corner. The "fables" we have been warned of in the Bible have now become our doctrine.

In Fundamentalism we have our "Holy Grails" which often are programs of every sort. One program which seems to have caught on with great popularity is Reformers Unanimous or better known as RU. While this program is not as extreme as others in the area of spiritual warfare, it is in error nonetheless. But its greatest danger lies in its promotional materials which, much like the modern day spiritual warfare movement, undermines the local church. In the RU promotions, they speak of the pastor not having the answer for the "addicted" and that he didn't know how to help. But has God not properly equipped the local church? Did God miss something? Was God's answer "a special deliverance program?" Of course not, but just as with Reformers Unanimous, the modern day spiritual warfare movement would have you to believe that there is a need for "specialists", "counselors", and other "better trained" people.

Part of the reason for the receptivity to spiritual warfare as well as other "helps" programs is that many in "Fundamentalism" have been blessed to have been saved at a very young age. It would be wonderful if all could have been. But when those saved at a young age encounter the ugliest side of our sin nature, they are shell-shocked. They are not used to dealing with many things that others are all too familiar with.

They become desperate, and while well-meaning, embrace just about anything in order to help these people. There is nothing more frightening than to be encountered with such tragedies, yet at the same time no greater opportunity to seek God's counsel.

One reason that others in the church recognize the errors of these programs is because when they were truly saved and submitted to God's Word, they were delivered from such sins. They were able to be free in Christ without the necessity of these programs. There are many Scriptural examples of people delivered and changed once they came to know Christ. One example would be Paul, one of the greatest persecutors of the church, who became one of its greatest champions. Many church splits have come from the embracing of para-church organizations that claim to have the answer that the local church cannot provide.

Regrettably, in some cases this is true. Not because God has not provided the answer, but that we are too busy pursuing other things. Unfortunately, these are the wrong things. But this does not justify embracing error. Are not the local church and the pastor, as well as the believer, well equipped enough to handle anything that comes their way? The answer is that with Christ all things are possible.

The real enemies are not the people in the modern day spiritual warfare movement nor those in our many personal help programs. The real enemy is the world, the flesh, and the devil. But those enemies are using our very desire to fix things by supplying us with tools that only make the problem worse.

Another real enemy is that because of the confusion created due to easy-believism, there are people trying to deal with unbelievers as believers and attempting to use Godly solutions on the lost.

> *I Corinthians 2:14 "But the natural man receiveth not the things of the Spirit of God: for they are foolishness unto him: neither can he know them, because they are spiritually discerned."*

It has been said that many well meaning people may be attempting to get a lost person to act like a saved person. The problem lies in that they are doing just that - acting. And eventually the act gets old and they go back to their old lifestyle since they attempted to change under their own power. It is the belief of many that the churches are full of lost people. If we were to make that decision based on the fruit on the tree, as well as the things we still struggle with, then this may be more accurate than once thought.

Believers still have the world, the flesh, and the devil to reckon with. The difference is that we have the indwelling Holy Spirit of God and His help in dealing with those three enemies.

Another real enemy is false teaching. We have succumbed to experience based, as well as world based theologies. There was a fine young evangelist who was being challenged regarding his belief in modern day spiritual warfare. His answer was quite self-convicting when he answered "How then do you explain what I saw?" There will not always be an answer to our questions here on earth and that is another part of the flesh that we wrestle with daily.

> *Deuteronomy 29:29 "The secret things belong unto the LORD our God: but those things which are revealed belong unto us and to our children for ever, that we may do all the words of this law."*

There will obviously be some things even within the realm of spiritual warfare that we will not understand, but if God has not chosen to show us, then we obviously need to trust God and accept it. The answer is not to create an answer. This seems to be one of the greatest errors. In our efforts rather than God's, we have tried to be as God and create an answer. The epidemic is spreading and is sure to do great harm to the cause of Christ. There is a cure as well as a true method to spiritual warfare. That cure will be found in the last chapter of this book. It is time to stop this epidemic and focus on what God would have us to do.

The enemy is real and should be confronted as we are Scripturally instructed; no other way will help, but will only spread the epidemic.

CHAPTER SIX

The Cure and the Consequences

John 14:6 "Jesus saith unto him, I am the way, the truth, and the life: no man cometh unto the Father, but by me."

It would seem that this verse has been lost in the shuffle of programs and spiritual warfare. When we seek a cure, we have The Great Physician who is the only way. In researching the reality of spiritual warfare, there are several solid conclusions which can be declared.

- God is real
- Satan is a very real foe
- Jesus Christ defeated Satan at the cross
- Satan is thus a defeated foe once and for all
- There are such things as demons

- Demons are limited to outside influences and are a stumbling block to the believer as are the world and the flesh
- A born again believer cannot be controlled by a demon
- Jesus Christ is "the" answer in spiritual warfare
- Believers cannot blame demons for their actions
- We must beware of fables as well as the words used by the modern day spiritual warfare movement
- That the modern day spiritual warfare movement is a very real danger to believers as well as unbelievers

But the question remains. Is there such a thing as spiritual warfare today? In the Biblical sense the answer is yes. But what is the Biblical sense?

Ephesians 6:12-19 "For we wrestle not against flesh and blood, but against principalities, against powers, against the rulers of the darkness of this world, against spiritual wickedness in high places. Wherefore take unto you the whole armour of God, that ye may be able to withstand in the evil day, and having done all, to stand. Stand therefore, having your <u>loins girt about with truth</u>, and <u>having on the breastplate of righteousness</u>; And <u>your feet shod with the preparation of the gospel of peace</u>; <u>Above all, taking the shield of faith</u>, wherewith ye shall be able to quench all the fiery darts of the wicked. And take <u>the helmet of salvation</u>, and <u>the sword of the Spirit, which is the word of God</u>: Praying always with all prayer and supplication in the Spirit, and watching thereunto with all perseverance and supplication for all saints; And for me, that utterance may be given unto me, that I may open my *mouth boldly, <u>to make known the mystery of the gospel</u>,"*

It is in this last verse we see what Biblical spiritual warfare truly is. That truth is that we may make known the mystery of the Gospel. Many will try to lay claim to part of Matthew 10:8 where the disciples are told to "cast out devils." But once again, the entire verse within its context is neglected.

> *Matthew 10: 5-14 "These twelve Jesus sent forth, and commanded them, saying, Go not into the way of the Gentiles, and into any city of the Samaritans enter ye not: But go rather to the lost sheep of the house of Israel. And as ye go, preach, saying, The kingdom of heaven is at hand. Heal the sick, cleanse the lepers, raise the dead, cast out devils: freely ye have received, freely give. Provide neither gold, nor silver, nor brass in your purses, Nor scrip for your journey, neither two coats, neither shoes, nor yet staves: for the workman is worthy of his meat. And into whatsoever city or town ye shall enter, enquire who in it is worthy; and there abide till ye go thence. And when ye come into an house, salute it. And if the house be worthy, let your peace come upon it: but if it be not worthy, let your peace return to you. And whosoever shall not receive you, nor hear your words, when ye depart out of that house or city, shake off the dust of your feet."*

Some will say that this verse, as well as the references to the seventy, justifies casting out demons. But the twelve were an elite group of which there are no members today as well as the seventy who were sent to prepare the way for the Lord's ministry. The ministry of the seventy was a temporary ministry and we do not have a direct contextual continuance of that group today. But if we are to equate their ministry to modern day spiritual warfare, then we cannot cherry pick from the verse. The verse instructed those to "Heal the sick, cleanse the lepers, raise the dead, cast out devils." Will the spiritual warfare movement not fulfill the full command? Are they healing the sick? Are they cleansing the lepers? Are they raising the dead? Of course not! Neither are they casting out devils.

Are they willing to "Provide neither gold, nor silver, nor brass in your purses, Nor scrip for your journey, neither two coats, neither shoes, nor yet staves: for the workman is worthy of his meat."?

No, that would seem to be too radical for them. But what can be more radical than modern day spiritual warfare? One might also question the financial motivation behind some of these "counselors." Unbiblical spiritual warfare has its consequences as has been previously discussed. One example of those consequences comes from one of the very passages those of the movement embrace as evidence in their favor.

> *I Samuel 28:7-16 "Then said Saul unto his servants, Seek me a woman that hath a familiar spirit, that I may go to her, and enquire of her. And his servants said to him, Behold, there is a woman that hath a familiar spirit at Endor. And Saul disguised himself, and put on other raiment, and he went, and two men with him, and they came to the woman by night: and he said, I pray thee, divine unto me by the familiar spirit, and bring me him up, whom I shall name unto thee. And the woman said unto him, Behold, thou knowest what Saul hath done, how he hath cut off those that have familiar spirits, and the wizards, out of the land: wherefore then layest thou a snare for my life, to cause me to*

die? And Saul sware to her by the LORD, saying, As the LORD liveth, there shall no punishment happen to thee for this thing. Then said the woman, Whom shall I bring up unto thee? And he said, Bring me up Samuel. And when the woman saw Samuel, she cried with a loud voice: and the woman spake to Saul, saying, Why hast thou deceived me? for thou art Saul. And the king said unto her, Be not afraid: for what sawest thou? And the woman said unto Saul, I saw gods ascending out of the earth. And he said unto her, What form is he of? And she said, An old man cometh up; and he is covered with a mantle. And Saul perceived that it was Samuel, and he stooped with his face to the ground, and bowed himself. And Samuel said to Saul, Why hast thou disquieted me, to bring me up? And Saul answered, I am sore distressed; for the Philistines make war against me, and God is departed from me, and answereth me no more, neither by prophets, nor by dreams: therefore I have called thee, that thou mayest make known unto me what I shall do. Then said Samuel, Wherefore then dost thou ask of me, seeing the LORD is departed from thee, and is become thine enemy?"

Note should be taken to "And when the woman saw Samuel, she cried with a loud voice." It seems that even the witch was shocked to have been able to conjure up Samuel. God allowed something that God had forbidden, and Saul was judged for his error in dealing with the occult. Saul failed to obey God's command.

Deuteronomy 18:10-13 "There shall not be found among you any one that maketh his son or his daughter to pass through the fire, or that useth divi-

nation, or an observer of times, or an enchanter, or a witch, Or a charmer, or a <u>consulter with familiar spirits</u>, or a wizard, or a necromancer. For all that do these things are an abomination unto the LORD: and because of these abominations the LORD thy God doth drive them out from before thee. Thou shalt be perfect with the LORD thy God."

But it seems that the modern day spiritual warfare movement is doing the same things when they question demons and consult them.[21] Saul suffered a great consequence for his actions.

I Chronicles 10:13 So Saul died for his transgression which he committed against the LORD, even against the word of the LORD, which he kept not, <u>and also for asking counsel of one that had a familiar spirit, to enquire of it;</u>

Are the modern day spiritual warfare counselors exempt from God's command? The answer is no. And it is very likely that many of them as well as the counselees have paid and will continue to pay a price for their dabbling with demons. One possible explanation regarding their interactions with demons could be the very thing that happened to Saul. God may be allowing it as a judgment on those who choose to defy God in this area.

But there truly is a modern day equivalent to the command of the twelve and of the seventy, and it is found later in the Gospel of Matthew. And indeed it can be performed today. It is a command that applies to the entire body of Christ. If one wants to perform true Biblical spiritual warfare, one only needs to follow Matthew 28:18-20.

Matthew 28:18-20 "And Jesus came and spake unto them, saying, All power is given unto me in heaven and in earth. Go ye therefore, and teach all nations, baptizing them in the name of the Father, and of the Son, and of the Holy Ghost: Teaching them to observe all things whatsoever I have commanded you: and, lo, I am with you alway, even unto the end of the world. Amen."

This verse addresses every issue in Matthew 10:8. Sin is a sickness that can be healed by accepting Christ and submitting your all to Him. Leprosy is a Biblical typology of sin, a sin which is healed by accepting Christ and submitting your all to Him. Lost people are dead in their trespasses and sin and can be raised again by accepting Christ as Savior and submitting their all to Him. And lastly, the true way to cast a devil out of one is for that person to accept Christ and submit their all to Him.

- There are no demons in believers nor can there be.
- A demon is unable to control a believer's actions no matter what a believer does.
- A believer sins because he has chosen to rebel against God and His Word.
- Sin is not a disease, a mental condition, or even an addiction.
- Sin is lack of submission to God. It is called rebellion.

Are there outside influences? Of course there are. But they are outside and only influences that each person must "choose" to act upon. True spiritual warfare exists in the daily life of every believer. As long as one chooses to obey God's will in his life, he is actively involved in spiritual warfare. The most important aspect of spiritual warfare is soulwinning.

This is an aspect that can truly set others free. Regrettably this aspect is being replaced by the modern day "artificial" spiritual warfare movement. Satan is a counterfeiter and it seems that one of his greatest counterfeits is being circulated in our churches today.

That counterfeit is the spiritual warfare movement. May the Lord open our eyes to the true battle ahead!

> *Hebrews 12:1-2 " Wherefore seeing we also are compassed about with so great a cloud of witnesses, let us lay aside every weight, and the sin which doth so easily beset us, and let us run with patience the race that is set before us, Looking unto Jesus the author and finisher of our faith; who for the joy that was set before him endured the cross, despising the shame, and is set down at the right hand of the throne of God."*

> *I Corinthians 1:22- 29 "For the Jews require a sign, and the Greeks seek after wisdom: But we preach Christ crucified, unto the Jews a stumblingblock, and unto the Greeks foolishness; But unto them which are called, both Jews and Greeks, Christ the power of God, and the wisdom of God. Because the foolishness of God is wiser than men; and the weakness of God is stronger than men. For ye see your calling, brethren, how that not many wise men after the flesh, not many mighty, not many noble, are called: But God hath chosen the foolish things of the world to confound the wise; and God hath chosen the weak things of the world to confound the things which are mighty; And base things of the world, and things which are despised, hath God*

chosen, yea, and things which are not, to bring to nought things that are: That no flesh should glory in his presence."

May we all preach Christ! May we fight the good fight! May we fight the true fight! If you are a believer, you no longer need to be enslaved by the beliefs of the unbiblical spiritual warfare movement because you ARE free in Christ! The cure is freedom in Christ and in His Word! If you need to be freed from demons, then accept Christ! If you need to be freed from oppression, then accept Christ! If you have already, then surrender your all to Him! The modern day spiritual warfare movement produces bondage. Christ gives us freedom!

Conclusion

It has been established that the unbiblical modern day spiritual warfare movement at best is deceiving people and at its worst is guilty of demonic channeling. It is in many cases causing mental anguish and in some cases physical loss of life. There are no winners in this movement, only losers. There are no success stories, although that would not justify experience over God's truth if there were.

One would think that if this were legitimately of God and genuinely worked, then these "counselors" would have success in their own families. But some of the saddest stories are of the tragedies in the lives of the very counselors who could not make it work only because it is deceptive and unbiblical. There are several examples where the counselor, or exorcist for lack of a better word, would take his child to another exorcist because it wouldn't work for him. Yet these people would like to try their craft on you.

Many have seen the failures in the very families of the counselors and have been left to wonder "if it didn't work for the counselor who knows the techniques, what hope is there for me?". This quote was taken from a church member after their pastor's wife murdered her own daughter and then committed suicide. This daughter had spiritual warfare performed on her to no avail. This unbiblical movement is tearing down the very work of Christ. It is destroying the very creation of God.

Of note is the fact that until the unbiblical teaching is introduced to a church, no one has any demonic encounters or at least identifies their problems as such. This is because the movement is creating the need. But most ironic is the fact that upon abandoning this unbiblical teaching, the demonic manifestations disappear.

To follow the unbiblical spiritual warfare movement is to turn your back on God and His Holy Word. You cannot look at it any other way. But there is hope for you. That hope is to believe God's Word and trust Jesus. Trust Him for your salvation. Trust Him for your security. Trust Him with everything in your life.

Hebrews 13:5 "... for he hath said, I will never leave thee, nor forsake thee."

If you know of someone who is suffering from this false teaching, you can help deliver them by sharing God's Word regarding the errors of the unbiblical spiritual warfare movement.

Bibliography

All Bible Quotations are taken from the King James Bible

Online Bible Quotations from the Online Bible versions of Barnes New Testament Notes, Jamieson, Fausset, Brown Commentary and Strong's Concordance by permission of onlinebible.net. Winterbourne, Ontario, Canada Timnathserah Inc., 2005

Anderson, Neil., The Bondage Breaker Eugene, OR: Harvest House Publishers 1993

Tucker Douglas E.. Spiritual Warfare (America's Stars & Stripes Ministries) date unknown

Curington, Steven R., Why is Everybody Crying? Rockford, Il, Boyd Stevens Publications, 2005

McDermott Mark R.http://www.museum.tv/archives/etv/F/htmlF/flipwilsons/flipwilsons.htm

Rugh Gil. Demonization of the Believer Lincoln, NE: Sound Words, 1994

Endnotes

1. Online Bible. Barnes Notes (Winterbourne, Ontario,: Timnathserah Inc.,, 2005) 2 Corinthians 10:4

2. Neil Anderson. The Bondage Breaker (Eugene, OR: Harvest House Publishers) p. 21

3. Ibid. p.41

4. Ibid. p. 9

5. Online Bible. Barnes Notes (Winterbourne, Ontario,: Timnathserah Inc.,, 2005) Matthew 12:43-45

6. Online Bible. Strong's Concordance (Winterbourne, Ontario,: Timnathserah Inc.,, 2005) Mark 5:15

7. Neil Anderson. The Bondage Breaker (Eugene, OR: Harvest House Publishers) p.19-20

8. Ibid. p. 20-21

9. Online Bible. Barnes Notes (Winterbourne, Ontario,: Timnathserah Inc.,, 2005) James 4:7

10. Douglas E. Tucker. Spiritual Warfare (America's Stars & Stripes Ministries) mentioned throughout tape series

11. Steven B. Curington. Why is Everybody Crying? International (Rockford, Il: Boyd Stevens Publications, 2005) p. 14

12. Douglas E. Tucker. Spiritual Warfare (America's Stars & Stripes Ministries) mentioned often tape series

13. Online Bible. Barnes Notes (Winterbourne, Ontario,: Timnathserah Inc.,, 2005) Acts 5:3

14. Online Bible, Jamieson, Faussett, Brown Commentary (Winterbourne, Ontario,: Timnathserah Inc.,, 2005) 2 Samuel 24:1

15. Douglas E. Tucker. Spiritual Warfare (America's Stars & Stripes Ministries) mentioned several times in audio tape series

16. Mark R. McDermott http://www.museum.tv/archives/etv/F/htmlF/flipwilsons/flipwilsons.htm

17. Gil Rugh. Demonization of the Believer (Lincoln, NE: Sound Words, 1994) p. 45

18. Steven B. Curington. Why is Everybody Crying? International (Rockford, Il: Boyd Stevens Publications, 2005) p. 61

19. Ibid. p. 62

20. Ibid. p. 69

21. It is common practice for the "Spiritual Warfare Counselor" to hold discussions with the demons and ask them questions thus gathering information regarding the counselee

Printed in the United States
55793LVS00002B/205-414